BECOMING THE ME I WANT TO BE

A Self-Help Guide to Building Self-Esteem

Don Simmermacher

R&E PUBLISHERS
SARATOGA, CALIFORNIA

R & E Publishers
P.O. Box 2008, Saratoga, CA 95070
Tel: (408) 866-6303   Fax: (408) 866-0825

Book Design by Diane Parker
Cover by Kaye Quinn

Library of Congress Card Catalog Number: 93-83490

ISBN 1-56875-055-2

CONTENTS

FOREWORD

My personal interest in self-image and self-esteem began over twenty years ago. I chose self-image and self-esteem as a topic for a Master's Thesis in Sociology. Not as much was known about self-image and self-esteem as there is today. I remember very vividly how difficult it was to get self-image and self-esteem approved as a thesis topic. My thesis advisor, who happened to be chairman of the Sociology Department, did not believe that self-image and self-esteem were worthy of serious academic study or would make a suitable research topic. After some discussion and assertive persuasion, I finally got my topic approved on condition. The condition was that I have a psychologist, an anthropologist, an educator, and a sociologist on my thesis committee. To make a long story short, I came out of my thesis orals knowing less about self-image and self-esteem than I thought I knew before my orals. Each committee member was coming from his/her own discipline angle and tended to spend the whole time arguing about the meaning and function of self-image and self-esteem and the various sources from which these self-functions arise.

Throughout the last decade, a plethora of new information regarding self-image and self-esteem has been made available. The self-esteem movement which has taken place over the last ten years has provided a wealth of new information to a wide range of people who have been curious about the role that self-image and self-esteem play in their everyday lives. Even with more information now being available on self-image and self-esteem, there is still no consensus regarding the true meaning of these terms. I, therefore, don't expect that all readers will agree with my interpretation and definition of self-image and self-esteem; but it is my hope that this book will at least generate more interest and thought concerning the subject.

No book is entirely the work of any one person, and that is true of this one. This book is the result of over ten years of work facilitating self-esteem enhancement seminars for such diverse groups as educators, counselors, social workers, business and industrial workers, medical personnel, and the general public. I am most grateful to the many hundreds of my self-esteem building workshop participants who, over the years, have helped me gain new insights, thoughts, and ideas about self-image and self-esteem; and it is these people who have provided most of the information that can be found in this book. I am also indebted to the many people in the human potential and self-esteem movements who have influenced the writing of this book.

It should be noted that this book was written primarily to be read and used by reasonably healthy, well-functioning people who are interested in better achieving their potential and building self-esteem. Though not intended to be the equivalent or substitute for conventional psychotherapy or mental health treatment, the proven exercises and activities found in this book provide a common-sense program designed to facilitate human growth and self-esteem. This book outlines a step-by-step systems approach to the setting and achievement of self-selected goals and will assist the reader to discover the incredible power that a positive self-image and authentic self-esteem has in promoting self-realization, self-fulfillment, and personal happiness.

PART ONE

Orientation to the nature, development and functions of self-image and self-esteem.

INTRODUCTION
PART ONE

A premise of this book is that the enhancement of self-esteem can be achieved through the process of self-actualization. Self-actualization is a term best identified with the renowned psychologist and author, Abraham Maslow. He is well known for his theory of self-actualization, and no attempt will be made in this writing to review his work in detail. The basic principle of self-actualization is that all human beings are motivated by a common set of fundamental values or needs. The goal of human striving and accomplishment is to "become the best that one can be," continually working to achieve one's human potential.

The self-actualization needs identified by Maslow are related to each other in the form of a hierarchy of lower to higher level needs. The basic needs and their priority as established by Maslow are listed as follows:

1. Physiological needs

2. Safety or security needs

3. Love, affection, and belonging needs

4. Self-esteem and self-worth needs

5. Self-actualization and self-realization needs

Maslow believed when these basic human needs were not met, the result is frustration or conflict. He believed that all people have a need to work toward attaining their potential, to develop talents and to achieve personal goals. Every individual is endowed with unique aptitudes, talents, abilities, and natural inclinations which must be fulfilled. Self-actualization may be thought of as achieving self-fulfillment and self-realization through living one's values and arriving at personally selected life goals which is the foundation upon which this book is built. The program outlined in this book is further based on the premise that people will never become fully self-actualized or exhaust all of their human potentials, but they can continually move from self-defeating to self-actualizing behavior.

This book is divided into two parts. Part One deals with an orientation to the nature, development, and functions of self-image and self-esteem in everyday life. Part Two describes and utilizes a systems approach to human development. The system is made up of four steps or functions leading to the building of a more positive self-image and self-esteem through the process of self-actualization. The four system functions are designed so that each individual function builds on the other, thereby providing a logical and orderly process for human growth and change. The four functions are described in detail in Part Two of this book.

A DEFINITION OF SELF-IMAGE
AND SELF-ESTEEM

"Make It Thy Business To Know Thyself" --Saavedra Cervantes

To fully understand the significance of self-esteem, it is equally important to comprehend the meaning of self-image. Trying to understand the concept of self-esteem without considering self-image is like trying to predict the weather without considering the temperature.

Webster partially defines image as a mental picture. Self-image is a mental picture we have of ourselves which can be either positive or negative. Self-image is a belief system we construct about ourselves which includes how we think and feel about ourselves as a person. Self-esteem, on the other hand, connotes positive thoughts and feelings about ourselves. Self-esteem includes feelings of self-acceptance, self-worth, self-respect, self-regard, self-confidence, self-reliance, and self-trust.

Self-image is a more general term than self-esteem. Everyone has a self-image but may not have self-esteem. Self-esteem means having a positive image of self. A negative self-image reflects the absence of self-esteem. Some have defined self-esteem as "a quiet confidence in one's own potential."

A main factor differentiating humans from other living organisms is that man is a conceptual being—as human beings, we can conceptualize self. We can define who we are and then decide if we like our identity or not. We can attach a value to self and the most important value is the value of self-worth. Without internalizing the value of self-worth, self-esteem cannot become a reality.

Self-esteem requires a sense of self-acceptance. Self-acceptance does not mean to be without a wish to change or improve. To find life reasonably satisfying, we must have an adequate and realistic self-image—a wholesome self-esteem. We must know ourselves, both our potentials and limitations, and be honest with ourselves concerning both. Our self-image must be a reasonable approximation of our true selves—being neither more than we are or less than we are. I believe this is what Shakespeare meant when he said, "To thine ownself be true; And it must follow as the night the day, thou canst not then be false to any man."

PRIMARY SOURCES OF SELF-IMAGE AND SELF-ESTEEM

"A positive self-image and healthy self-esteem is based on approval, acceptance and recognition from others; but also upon actual accomplishments, achievements and success and upon the realistic self-confidence which ensues"   --Abraham Maslow

As Maslow points out in the above quote, there are basically two sources of self-esteem. One is external which relies on social responses from others. Social systems such as families, schools, and the work place provide social responses influencing the acquisition of self-image and self-esteem. The other is an internal origin of self-image and self-esteem which involves direct experiences in personal goal achievement. We have more control over internal sources of self-esteem because external sources require relying on others whereas internal sources arise from individual choice and personal action (self-actualization).

Those who have an excessive need for approval, acceptance, and recognition may actually jeopardize self-esteem. They may become so submissive and conforming towards others that they lose touch with their own individuality. Such persons may be unable to distinguish between the genuine self and the counterfeit self. Those who set a goal to be liked and accepted by everyone will experience little knowledge of who they are and will pay the price of loss of self-esteem, personal integrity, and self-regard.

It is evident that we are not born with a self-image. Self-image is learned. Webster's definition of *learned* is: "To come to realize, to become informed, to gain knowledge or understanding." To gain knowledge or understanding of self is the true objective of self-discovery. The "self" has not been a subject of learning. Self-discovery has not been seen as an academic goal and has usually been discouraged. (Our schools do not offer Introspection 101.) A question I've often considered, both as a teacher and counselor, is why should we have to be a candidate for psychotherapy to learn about self? Maybe if we learned about self, we wouldn't need psychotherapy.

SELF-ESTEEM
IS NOT CONCEIT

"Until I accept my faults, I will certainly doubt my virtues"

--Hugh Prather

There is a great difference between conceit and self- esteem. A conceited person feels inferior and uses the defense of compensation to cover up perceived weaknesses. You can accept your accomplishments and achievements without conveying that you are better than others or acting superior. If you have authentic self-esteem, you have no need to falsely impress others and you will come across as you really are—namely, a self-confident and self-reliant person who knows who you are and what you want out of life. A person with a positive self-image does not resort to bravado or being a "grandstander." Conceit and self-centeredness are a result of a negative image of self, not a positive one. Bragging and acting the "big shot" is really a form of false self-esteem rather than authentic self-worth.

Egotism does not come from having too much ego, but from having too little. Egotism is sometimes confused with self-acceptance. Egotism is not healthy self-acceptance but is symptomatic of self-rejection and self-hate. Egotism involves an exaggerated or excessive preoccupation with self to the exclusion of others. This form of egotistical behavior is an attempt to gain reassurance—to compensate for a negative self-image and low self-esteem.

THE IMPORTANCE OF SELF-IMAGE AND SELF-ESTEEM IN DAILY LIVING

"So much is a man worth as he esteems himself"

--Francois Rebalais

Our self-image (how we think and feel about ourselves as a person) determines how we act, how we learn, how we work, how we play, and how we relate to others. Our level of self-esteem determines how we cope with problems in living and fulfill our needs. Self-esteem involves a sense of self-confidence and self-reliance in our ability to meet the challenges of life.

In building self-esteem, we need to look at what's right with us, not just what's wrong. We need to acknowledge our potential self. Many of us have been conditioned since childhood by false self-concepts and beliefs which have kept us from achieving self-worth and self-esteem. Unless we learn to perceive our own true worth as a person, we cannot come close to achieving a positive self-image.

The need for a positive identity and self-esteem is common to all of us. This need includes the fundamental achievement of self-acceptance, self-confidence, self-reliance, self-worth, and self-respect. It is no exaggeration to state that acquiring a positive self-image and authentic self-esteem is essential for positive human growth and healthy personal adjustment. It is important to know that our image of self is always subject to change despite the past. No single event or person can determine the level of one's self-esteem. Self-esteem develops over time and is always subject to change. Learning to value oneself, having high self-esteem and self-acceptance, can happen to anyone. Learning to accept ourselves and making the most of that self is an important step in building self-esteem. When we are willing to work to achieve our human potential, we are on the right track to building a more positive self-image and self-esteem.

SELF-ESTEEM AND SELF-DEVELOPMENT

"We know what we are,but know not what we may be"

--William Shakespeare

Self-development means finding your own sense of identity. One who is a stranger to self is unable to experience the great personal satisfaction of achieving human potential. Self-development means finding your own purpose for living—it means tapping your deepest potentials—it means becoming the total person you want to become. James Fadiman in his book, "Unlimit Your Life," states that "only to the degree that you can truly acknowledge your unique human potential will you be free of your self-imposed limitations."

The development of your potentialities and the process of self-discovery never ends. Most of us go through life being only partially aware of our full range of talents and abilities. Self-development is a human growth process that you can pursue and keep pursuing throughout your total life. You can continue to seek and discover a full range of human potentials that can be tapped, developed, and utilized as long as you may live.

In the process of self-development, we may sometimes encounter personal failure. Failures are an inevitable part of everyone's life, and we must learn to take our failures in stride while enjoying our achievements and accomplishments. Dwelling on past mistakes and failures serves no good purpose and only tends to diminish self-esteem. We need to learn from our mistakes and failures and then let them go. The real key to success is not to never fail, but rather to learn as much as possible from our failures so that we can avoid repeating them. As John Gardner states, "We pay a heavy price for our fear of failure. It is a powerful obstacle to growth. There is no learning without some difficulty and fumbling. If you want to keep learning, you must keep risking all your life."

Willingness to take reasonable risks can bolster self-esteem. Taking calculated risks offer more than just the chance to fail. Risks can bring potential gain, success, pleasure, pride, and an increased sense of self-confidence and self-esteem. People with a positive self-image are willing to take reasonable risks. A risk well chosen stretches your limits and helps you to achieve your true potential. Risks often times may require moving beyond your comfort zone. Staying the way you are may be painful but seen as the path of least resistance. The old adage "nothing ventured, nothing gained" holds true.

If you accept no risks, you will become a spectator in life instead of being the active player you could be. Without the self-image strength to assume some risks, you will remain on the sidelines of life.

SELF-ESTEEM AND HUMAN RELATIONS

"As you love yourself, so shall you love others. Strange but true, but with no exceptions"   --Harry Stack Sullivan

How you perceive yourself as a person—your image of self—determines, in large part, how well you relate to others. If you've developed a negative image of yourself, you will hesitate to seek out close and caring relationships with others. If you see yourself as inferior, you will find relationships with others to be threatening and frightful. Not liking yourself, you will have trouble believing that others will like and accept you.

If, on the other hand, you see yourself as a person with self-confidence and self-worth, you will be willing to seek out and establish meaningful and sustaining relationships with others. You will be free to accept yourself as you are and accept others as they are.

Self-acceptance is absolutely essential for the acceptance of others. Respect for others begins with respect for self. Loving ourselves is a basic requirement in establishing loving relationships with others.

People often tend to gravitate to other people who will re-inforce their own self-image. If we have a negative self-image, we will likely seek out others with low self-esteem. The old saying that "misery loves company" seems to be true. If you are involved with people who tend to drag you down, you should be concerned. People who try to drag others down are people who don't like themselves and are critical of themselves and others. They tend to complain about most things and see themselves as life failures. One cannot sustain good feelings and cheerfulness when in their company. Their negative and pessimistic attitude takes the fun and excitement out of life. They are generally unhappy, unfulfilled, anxious and lonely individuals who have lost trust in themselves and their ability to establish trusting relationships with others.

If one is to maintain a positive self-image and self-esteem, he/she will find it in his/her best interest to sever his/her relationships with self-destructive individuals. Those with a negative self-image can have a negative effect on the people with whom they are involved. Positive self-image people do not allow others to bring them down or rob them of their own dignity, self-esteem, or self-respect.

SELF-ESTEEM AND
THE POTENTIAL SELF

"Compared to what we could be, we are only half awake. We are making use of only a small part of our physical and mental resources. The human individual lives far within his limits. He possesses powers of various sorts which he habitually fails to use"   --William James

Human potential advocates such as Abraham Maslow, Gordon Allport, Rollo May, Herbert Otto, and others suggest that most of us are functioning at a small fraction of our human potential. Webster partially defines potential as: "the possible but not yet realized capacity for growth and development or coming into being." Some say that just existing is sufficient for self-esteem. I tend to disagree. Sleep walking through life or living in a serenity trance does not enhance self-esteem. Authentic self-esteem comes from achieving our human potential—from becoming what we can become.

A key to achieving our human potential is finding our own niche in life—what I call "show through" talents. We all have unique potentials. We are all born gifted in our own way. We need to find out what is special about us and build on our special talents and abilities. Any developed skill boosts our overall sense of self-esteem and encourages a willingness to take on new life challenges with self-confidence, self-trust, and self-reliance.

Poor self-esteem causes people to accept far less than what they could be. Unsure of our potentials, we are often willing to settle for second best rather than becoming the person we could be. We should investigate and accept ourselves as nature made us, but also realize that nature gave us the potential to grow. Jean Paul Sarte stated that "We are our choices." We are responsible for choosing the person we are today and we are responsible for choosing the person we wish to become tomorrow. When we learn what and who we are, we will be better able to think about what and who we wish to become—both as unique individuals and growing human beings. Achieving human potential may not be easy, but with effort, it is always possible.

SELF-ESTEEM AND THE POSTPONED LIFE

"You are the only one who can use your ability—that is an awesome responsibility"   --Ralph Waldo Emerson

Many people seem to put life on hold with no future goals or expectations—just live from day to day or go with the flow with no hope for a better future. Our future will be the same as our past unless we do something to change it. Although we know that we can change and grow, changing requires a conscious choice and a great deal of effort. If we keep doing what we're doing, we keep getting what we're getting. Many of us don't want to make the necessary effort to change and continue to feel frustrated, unfulfilled, and insignificant. We need to stop doing the things that lower self-esteem and start doing more things to raise self-esteem.

Achieving human potential does not mean trying to become perfect. Striving for excellence is one thing, expecting to achieve perfection is quite another. Perfectionism is a compulsion that tends to lower self-esteem. Perfectionists are always looking for something wrong, both in themselves and in others. Since nothing in life is totally perfect, perfectionists are frequently frustrated, disappointed, and angry. It is difficult for perfectionists to accept themselves or others as they are and they are very critical of themselves and others. Perfectionists are their own worst enemies. They believe that unless they are faultless, they are worthless— they are never good enough in their own eyes.

Neurotic perfectionism should not be confused with the healthy pursuit of human growth and self-esteem. To avoid perfectionism, we need to avoid the negative self-talk that says, "I'm not good enough if I'm not perfect."

If you are a perfectionist, you will find your self-esteem going up by having the courage to be imperfect and to accept human limitations in yourself as well as in others.

SELF-ESTEEM AND SELF-ACTUALIZATION

"Those who believe they can do something and those who believe they can't are both right"   --Henry Ford

Self-actualization means being able to make decisions based on what is important to you and taking action on those decisions. Self-actualization requires setting goals—goals allow us to determine and create our own future. Having goals means to work towards a new destination in human growth, self-direction, and self-esteem.

The renowned psychologist and author, Abraham Maslow, coined the term self-actualization and described the self-actualized individual as one who excels in living. According to Maslow, each person has a desire to maximize his/her human potential—to become what he/she can become.

We cannot become self-actualized or develop self-esteem without personal initiative and self-reliance. Self-actualization is defined as achieving in action. All people have a need to work toward attaining their potential, to develop talents, and to achieve personal goals. Self-esteem is built on personal initiative and accomplishment. Without personal initiative and the belief that we can be self-actualizing, genuine self-confidence and authentic self-esteem is all but impossible to achieve. As the noted psychiatrist and author Leon Tec states, "Self-esteem is built on accomplishment, on the ability to solve problems, and to accomplish what we set out to accomplish. Without a sense of accomplishment, without the feeling that we can be effective in our behavior, genuine self-confidence and self-esteem is all but impossible. And without confidence and self-esteem, our capacity to derive joy and satisfaction from the life process itself is all but crippled."

Self-actualization and achieving potential is not an accident—it is the result of intelligent effort and personal action. Self-actualization is an on-going process. Those who believe they have become totally self-actualized have lost sight of their goals, or perhaps never really saw them in the first place.

THE POWER OF
CHOICE

"The freedom to make choices and to learn from them is the core of being and the basis of all individuality" --Clark E. Moustakas

Throughout life, we are faced with countless choices. The choice of a vocation, the choice of a relationship, the choice to remain at a job or find a new one, the choice to marry or stay single, the choice to have children are all examples of choices we all make in our everyday lives.

There are a lot of books out today that tell us that we are all just victims of circumstances and that life is basically controlled by outside or external forces of which we have no control. This idea is especially espoused in much of the so called "new age" literature. The new age movement does not leave much room for more rational approaches to human growth and development.

As a counselor, I have worked with many clients who have agonized over making decisions and choices in their lives. Some of them became so anxious and distressed about making a choice that they would ask me to make the choice for them. I would then remind them that my role as a counselor was to help them identify alternatives, but that the choice was ultimately their responsibility. Some would then respond by complaining that seeing more alternatives only made the choice more difficult. I would then counter by reminding them that having more options really gave them more freedom in making the best choice to solve their dilemma.

Some people, especially those with low self-esteem, avoid making choices because they are afraid to take a risk or accept a challenge. These people tend to see the making of choices as a frightening, risky, and painful process. This fear and anticipatory anxiety render them unwilling to make the choices to get what they really want out of life.

Making choices requires that we know who we are and what we want. In my self-esteem enhancement seminars, the first two steps made are to conceptualize self and clarify values. Conceptualizing self is primarily designed to assist training group participants to identify their human potentials and limitations. Knowing who you are, realizing your "potential self," can provide greater self-confidence, self-reliance, and self-trust in making life choices.

Knowing your values is also important in making decisions and choices. Most all decisions and choices involve values. Our values guide our choices and actions. When we are unable to make choices, it is usually because we are experiencing value conflicts. Deciding which values are most important to us can reduce the value conflicts in our lives. Making choices requires that we examine and prioritize values. We cannot make rational choices without knowing what values are most important to us. Making our own choices increases our autonomy and freedom, and once acted upon, can give us the power to shape our own destiny.

GOAL SETTING AND SELF-ESTEEM

"Those who set goals create their own futures"

--James Fadiman

Goal achievement plays an integral part in building self-esteem. Goals that are specific, realistic, meaningful, and measurable and are in line with our own potentials and limitations can reflect a full awareness of who we are. Achieving self-selected goals based on your own beliefs and values reinforces and enhances your self-esteem. Goal accomplishments give you a sense of personal fulfillment and self-pride. Recognizing your own efforts in the goal achievement process increases your self-confidence, self-determination, and self-motivation. Setting a goal implies a belief in yourself to achieve it and expresses an attitude of optimism about life and your chances for success.

Goals allow us to focus on meaningful targets which give us something to aim for. People without goals have very vague notions of who they are and what they want out of life. Goal achievements can reinforce our beliefs and values and help us gain significant insight about ourselves and our self-image.

The reason many people fail to set goals is that they have never really learned how important it is to set goals and have never been given guidance in the goal setting process. Many are afraid of both real and sometimes imagined goal obstacles that they may encounter. Some see goal obstacles as fearful and threatening rather than an exciting life challenge. Sometimes the achievement of a goal can be blocked by internal factors such as our own feelings of inadequacy or lack of self-confidence. Often it is our own expectation of goal failure that creates the failure. To overcome these internal blocks, we must learn to change the negative thoughts, feelings, and attitudes about ourselves and learn to realistically assess our own true potential talents and capabilities.

Goal obstacles can also be external such as those coming from other people or outside extenuating circumstances over which we have little or no control. If the blocks or obstacles are coming from external factors, we may need to reassess these factors and identify realistic approaches or strategies to overcome or bypass them. Since one of the criterion for goal setting is that the goal be realistic, we will need to anticipate and plan for goal obstacles before we set the goal.

Achieving a worthwhile goal can increase feelings of self-worth and self-esteem. All of us have experienced goal accomplishments that have made us feel good about ourselves.

This sounds so obvious as to be unworthy of further discussion. Some people, however, are confused or have misconceptions regarding the relationship between goal achievement and self-esteem enhancement. For instance, striving for goal accomplishment as a means of fostering superiority or triumphs over others can contribute to false self-esteem. Goal accomplishments that are motivated by a need for self-glorification or self-aggrandizement can diminish self-esteem. Seeking goals just for attention or recognition may stem from feelings of inadequacy, worthlessness, or inferiority. People working towards a more positive self-image do not need public praise or adulation. They do not need trophies or medals and do not seek them. Instead, they seek goal achievement just for the fun of it, for the good feelings that come with self-realization and human growth, for the joy and personal satisfaction that accompanies self-accomplishment. Goal achievement can and should be seen as its own reward. As James Hall states in his book on goal setting, "The key to goal setting is first to set the goal and then enjoy the journey."

SELF-RESPONSIBILITY, SELF-CONTROL, AND SELF-EMPOWERMENT

"Man's self-concept is enhanced when he takes responsibility for himself"
                                                            --William Shutz

Responsibility is defined as the ability to respond. We almost always have the choice of how to respond to life situations. People must accept responsibility for their own lives and the fulfillment of their needs. Each individual is responsible for finding his/her own meaning and purpose in life. Each is responsible for taking control over his/her own life. Taking control of one's life takes understanding, determination, and sincere effort. Taking control of your life requires understanding the relationships between your human potentials and limitations, your beliefs and values, and your goals and objectives.

Many people tend to suggest that they need to let go when what they really need to do is to take hold. They do not need to surrender self but rather need to strengthen and expand self—to seek self-empowerment rather than self-resignation.

Self-empowerment means to have a sense of personal power, self-efficacy, and self-direction. Self-empowerment also means having control over your life without the need to change and control the lives of those around you. Self-empowerment requires having positive and realistic feelings and attitudes about yourself—it means liking and accepting yourself as a competent and capable person. Self-empowerment requires finding your own special purpose for living. Self-empowerment means working to become the person you want to become. Only to the degree that you can acknowledge your unique human potential will you develop the self-empowerment to overcome your self-imposed limitations.

SELF-TRUST AND SELF-CHANGE

"Self-trust is the first secret of success"

--Ralph Waldo Emerson

Having a sense of self-trust requires that people know their true selves, not a deceptive self-image. Failure to truly know one's self can stifle positive self-image change and human growth. The authors of the book, "Take 10 to Grow," make reference to two factors influencing resistance to self-image change which are (1) self-talk and (2) selective perceptions.

Self-Talk refers to what we tell ourselves about ourselves. Negative self-talk is a kind of demeaning self-discussion. When we put ourselves down by belittling or berating ourselves, we are contributing to and reinforcing a negative self-image. Negative self-talk is a form of irrational thinking about yourself which leads to self-dislike and self-rejection. It follows, therefore, that a way to avoid a negative image of self is to change negative self-talk to positive self-talk. Positive self-talk requires the ability to think rationally about yourself and to forgive yourself for your human shortcomings, failures, and mistakes.

Selective Perceptions means perceiving what we expect or want to perceive. If you choose to perceive yourself as a worthless or inadequate person, you will tend to see only those things about yourself which reinforce this negative image of self. You will then be prone to rejecting or discounting experiences which argue against this negative self-belief and see only the things that substantiate it. Negative selective perceptions can contribute to the belief that you are unable to change, to grow, to learn, and to behave differently—the phrase "The me I see is the me I'll be" seems to hold true for most of us.

DISCOVERING THE REAL YOU

"Who can say more than this rich praise, that you alone are you?" --William Shakespeare

All of us have a self-image which contains both positive and negative traits. We all feel confident about some things and shaky about others. A young man, for example, may have high self-esteem about his athletic skills, while at the same time may feel less confident about his academic abilities. A woman may be quite proud of her professional skills as a nurse, but feel somewhat inadequate as a mother or wife; or she may feel that she has been a good homemaker or mother, but question her capabilities as a nurse, and so on. Having a negative image of self in some areas of our lives is quite common and should not be viewed as a character deficiency or disgraceful condition. To be overly troubled about our human deficiencies can, however, create serious problems in our everyday lives. We must accept the fact that we are imperfect beings in an imperfect world.

A way to destroy self-esteem is to always compare ourselves to others. There is always someone more capable in an area than we are. Few of us have such a monopoly on talent that no one else can do better. No two persons who ever lived were ever exactly alike. Although you may excel in some areas, so you will fall short in others. Some have to work hard to become proficient at something while others may excel with little effort. Comparing ourselves to others can prevent us from thinking and acting independently and keep us from achieving our unique human potentials. Since we are each unique individuals, there is no need to compare ourselves to others.

Thinking positively about yourself and knowing and believing that you have the potential to change for the better is the first step in building a more positive self-image—the first step to renewing self-regard and self-acceptance as a worthwhile human being. A positive regard for self requires the willingness to accept our human limitations while building on our unique human potentials. As stated earlier, achieving our potential is best accomplished through the process of self-actualization. Self-actualization requires that we be willing to see ourselves in new ways and assume the challenge of human growth. We must always remember that self-esteem develops over time and is constantly subject to change with new life experiences.

Though the concept of self may be rather elusive, we certainly experience the self as real. Most of us, unless suffering from some abnormality such as amnesia or multiple personality disorder, have some fairly definite notion of who we are. The self is not as vague or nebulous as some may think. After all, we never rush to the mirror and wonder who is going to be there. We must remember, however, that much of our self-image is a product of social responses and feedback from others and may be subject to distorted or faulty perceptions. Obtaining authentic self-awareness and a positive identity is necessary for both physical and psychological well being.

SELF-IMAGE, SELF-ESTEEM, AND THE SELF-IDEAL

"And there were three men
went down the road
as down the road went he
the man they saw, the man he was
and the man he wanted to be"   --John Masefield

The Self-Image is the picture we have of ourselves— how we think and feel about ourselves as a person. Self-Esteem means that one has a positive sense of self-worth and self-acceptance as a person. The Self-Ideal is the image a person has of the kind of person he or she would like to be. Though our self-image, self-esteem, and self-ideal can be considered separate components, these self-functions are highly interrelated and interdependent.

Raymond Gale sheds light on the self-ideal in the following: "When the self-ideal is founded upon a realistic assessment of one's own capacities and limitations, it can serve as a compass to guide the individual's behavior, his long-range goals, and his planning and implementation of aspirations—a road map for his effective living."

The self-ideal serves as a foundation for our personal values and philosophy of life—our aspirations and desired achievements. Our self-ideal provides a standard or norm by which we measure our own human growth and self-realization. When we believe we do not measure up to our self-ideal, we can develop feelings of personal disappointment and self-rejection.

It is most important that our self-ideal be both realistic and achievable. Unrealistically high aspirations can result in failure to live up to our self-ideal, whereas unrealistically low aspirations can deprive us of the opportunity of achieving our true potential. When we act in accordance with our realistic self-ideal, the sense of a positive identity tends to be reinforced. An unrealistic, rigid, and inflexible self-expectation, however, can produce a kind of "tyrannical" self-ideal that can lead to anxiety, stress, apprehension and guilt if not achieved.

The level of self-esteem is affected by the difference between the self-image and self-ideal. When the difference between the self-image and self-ideal is great, self-esteem will be lowered. The closer the self-ideal and the self-image, the higher the self-esteem. Though the self-image and self-ideal should be in close proximity, they should not be identical. Human growth requires that we continue striving for self-improvement. Throughout life, the overlap between the self-image and self-ideal will fluctuate which tends to define the bench mark by which we measure achievement, success, and self-accomplishment.

Failure to achieve one's self-ideal should never result in feelings of hopelessness or discouragement. The self-ideal should always be seen as a guideline to self-realization and not an absolute indicator of success or failure as a human being. By working to reach our self-ideal, we gain a greater sense of self-acceptance, self-pride, and self-respect.

THE NEED FOR HOPE

"Where there is life, there is hope; but also, where there is hope there is life"   --Karl Menninger

Hopelessness and despair are the result of our unfulfilled need to realize our own human potential. Mobilizing our potential toward human growth requires self-discovery and personal action. Self-discovery involves the ability and willingness to realistically look at ourselves and to know our human potentials and limitations. Self-discovery must also include insight regarding the ways in which we are meeting the challenges of life and fulfilling our needs. Along with self-discovery, we need to take personal action. We must be willing to identify and pursue goals leading from self-defeating behavior to growth-producing behavior. In the process of human growth, we must retain hope rather than hopelessness in our daily lives. To have self-esteem and positive self-regard, we must have the conviction that there is meaning and purpose to our lives. In order to live a happy, productive and fulfilling life, we must have hope for the future. Hope is not to be confused with wishful thinking or unrealistic expectations. Such hope may actually diminish self-esteem if it is based solely on unrealistic fantasies. Hope that is in keeping with realistic possibilities can generate self-actualization, self-determination, and self-empowerment. Lack of hope, on the other hand, can stifle the utilization of our human potential and perpetuate a condition of emptiness. As Rollo May points out in his classic book, *Man's Search for Himself*, "The human being cannot live in a condition of emptiness for very long; if he is not growing toward something, he does not merely stagnate; the pent-up potentialities turn into morbidity and despair, and eventually into destructive activities."

It is most satisfying and fulfilling to go through life spreading hope instead of despair, encouragement instead of discouragement, and love instead of hate. Hopelessness is the enemy of human growth and aliveness. Hope can make the difference between simply existing or living. Some people live in the gloomy dungeons of their own making and complain of the darkness, while others prefer to live in the light of meaning, purpose, and hope for their present and future lives.

OVERCOMING
POWERLESSNESS

"Man must accept the responsibility for himself and the fact that only by using his own powers can he give meaning to life"

--Erich Fromm

People with low self-esteem tend to believe they are powerless to improve their present and future lives. Those who harbor feelings of insecurity, vulnerability, and self-doubt tend to view the future with anxiety and trepidation while those with a greater sense of self-confidence and self-reliance see the future as an opportunity for personal challenge and growth.

Those who have a positive self-image and internalized self-esteem are willing to take responsibility for their own actions, accepting both the positive and negative consequences of their decisions, conduct, and behavior. Having the power of self-esteem, these people are able to choose among life alternatives and to determine their own destinies. People who lack a sense of positive self-reliance and self-direction tend to believe that their choices and actions have little or no influence on life events and that they are helpless victims of chance, circumstance or fate. These people tend to rely on fortuitous events, fate, luck, or even their astrological signs to determine what they believe to be their destinies in life.

In contrast, people with a positive self-image and self-reliance believe that they can exert a high level of influence and control over their present and future lives. They believe that they are, to a large degree, masters of their own fate and have the inner strength and self-determination to face life's challenges in an enthusiastic, optimistic and responsible manner. Positive self-image people accept themselves as creatures of choice and not just mindless instruments of external controlling forces. They know that they alone have the power of positive self-control that allows them the opportunity of fulfilling their own life values and goals.

We each have the power within us to choose happiness over unhappiness, self-fulfillment over self-defeat, and hope over despair. We are not pushed forward by mysterious or unconscious motivating forces from the past, but instead are pulled ahead by our own self-determined hopes, plans, and intentions for the future.

BUILDING AUTHENTIC SELF-ESTEEM

"To attain 'success' without attaining self-esteem is to be condemned to feeling like an imposter anxiously awaiting exposure"   --Nathaniel Branden

Throughout this book, I have stressed the importance of achievements, accomplishments, and success as a means of building authentic self-esteem. Why is it then that we sometimes see people who appear to be successful yet seem to lack self-esteem? This sounds like a paradox, but there are several reasons why this could be the case. Some people don't believe they deserve their success or haven't really earned it. People with low self-esteem often feel that they are frauds or imposters in some areas of their lives and fail to own their accomplishments and achievements. Despite evidence of success, some people remain convinced that they are not responsible for their own success. Success and achievement can be very personal. What one person regards as success, another may not.

Being a perfectionist can also be an obstacle to the appreciation of success. Perfectionists tend to underrate their accomplishments while overemphasizing their failures. Attributing success to factors other than one's own talents, abilities and efforts can keep one from internalizing success. Until achievements, accomplishments, and success can be owned, self-esteem will be jeopardized.

Compromising moral or ethical values can also diminish self-esteem. Sidney Simon, in his insightful book, *Getting Unstuck*, states that values are guides for daily living that influence your thoughts, feelings, actions, and deeds. They shape your personality and give direction to what would otherwise be an aimless, purposeless life. Your values are reflected in your goals, hopes, dreams, attitudes, interests, convictions, and behavior.

Knowing your values is important because you live by them and work for them. Your values determine what matters most to you and what is important to you. Your values hold the key to your self-determination and motivation. A direct relationship exists between your values and what you will be motivated to work for and achieve. Values determine and affect your life goals. Human growth may be defined as self-change in a valued direction.

As stated earlier, the most important value we can have is the value of self-worth. People with a negative self-image and low self-esteem are prone to minimizing their self-worth. Despite their accomplishments, they seem to acquire the habit of telling how little they amount to and how insignificant they are in comparison to others. The habit of self-depreciation and self-devaluation can leave one bankrupt as a person. Nothing becomes more valuable to a person than total self-acceptance and an unqualified endorsement of self. Self-esteem requires that we continue to recognize our own human uniqueness. We are the only one exactly like us in the world—with our own unique potentials, aptitudes, interests, and natural inclinations.

SELF-ESTEEM AND WELLNESS

"There is no illness of the body apart from the mind" --Socrates

The World Health Organization defines health as physical, social, and psychological well being. Few people realize that many of their ailments can be emotionally induced. Our self-image has a lot to do with both our physical and mental well being. When we allow ourselves to be governed by our emotions and moods, we can open the door to the enemies of our health, success, and happiness.

Most doctors can recall patients who, on being told they have a serious illness, seem to give up and soon wither and die, while others who refuse to accept the diagnosis live out their lives with unexplained energy, suffering less pain and fewer physical symptoms. There appears to be some truth to the adage, "If we think healthy thoughts, we attract health."

Holistic health and psychosomatic illness research indicates that there is no real scientific method to completely control for the interaction between mind (psyche) and body (soma), but there is reasonably good evidence to suggest that a person's mental state can contribute to disease.

A factor contributing to both physical and mental illness is stress. There are many people in the medical community today who would agree that stress is one of the biggest causal factors of disease and illness. Dr. Hans Selye, one of the most well-known researchers of stress, distinguishes between the stress of failure or frustration, which is harmful (distress), and other kinds of stress, such as life challenges, which he sees as beneficial or positive (eu-stress). This positive or eu-stress keeps us alert, challenged, and stimulated. Distress, on the other hand, can be both physically and mentally damaging. Selye believes that distress results in physical disabilities such as ulcers, tension headaches, allergies, digestive disorders, heart disease, high blood pressure, and strokes. Though Selye indicates that eu-stress may actually be good for us because without it, we'd lack the energy, enthusiasm, and motivation to act or respond to life's demands and challenges, he is quick to caution that distress can be dangerous to both our physical and mental well-being.

Stress is an inevitable part of life. Studies are now showing a direct relationship between self-image and stress. How we think and feel about ourselves (self-image) directly influences the way we react or respond to life stressors. Two major functions of the self-image are to assist one in coming to grips with inevitable life problems and to fulfill both physical and social needs. As negative self-image people experience failure in coping with life's problems and satisfying needs, they will likely experience strong feelings of distress. Most of the distress comes from the perceptions, meaning, and interpretations given to the situation and circumstances producing the distress. The manner in which individuals will define or interpret a stressful experience is very much related to their self-image and level of self-esteem. Adopting the right temperament and attitude toward self can have a profound effect on stress management. It is important to remember that all people experience stress, and it is up to each individual to determine his/her own stress level. As we continue our journey in the search for self-esteem, we will gain greater ability to constructively use positive stress while reducing the negative stress in our lives.

Studies are showing that people with a positive self-image and self-esteem seem to enjoy robust health, avoid debilitating disease, and deal more effectively with factors that can increase suscept-ibility to both physical and mental illness. Biofeedback machines that are designed to give audible or visual signals whenever physiological changes occur have helped us better understand more about the relationship between mind and body. The use of these machines has demonstrated that we can actually learn to control our bodies' processes mentally. Of course, much still needs to be learned about how mental factors actually affect physical health; but it would appear that having a positive self-image, self-confidence, and self-esteem can provide significant self-protection not only against mental but also against physical ills. Building a positive self-image and enhancing self-esteem may very well function as a kind of inexpensive health insurance.

WHO IS THE ENEMY?

"A person who doubts himself is like a man who would enlist in the ranks of his enemies and bear arms against himself"

--Alexandre Dumas

Who is the enemy? We carry him around with ourselves wherever we go. He robs us of our dignity, self-worth, hopes, and freedom. He destroys our potential for happiness, fulfillment, and human growth. He stands as a barrier between ourselves and other human beings. Who is the enemy? The enemy resides in all of us to some degree. The enemy is our own negative self-image and low self-esteem.

Our self-image can be our best friend or worst enemy depending on its strength or weakness. The need for a positive identity and healthy self-esteem is common to all human beings. This need includes the fundamental achievement of self-acceptance, self-respect, self-confidence, self-reliance, and self-worth. Knowing and believing that our self-image can change for the better is the first step in the human growth process. It is no exaggeration to state that acquiring a positive self-image and authentic self-esteem is essential to self-worth and healthy personal adjustment.

It is essential for self-esteem that we never forfeit appreciation for ourselves and our sense of self-worth. To maintain our self-approval, we must continue to work to achieve our values and human potential. If we keep our self-approval, no matter what other objects of value we may lose, we will still be rich. In an ever-changing and depersonalized world, we must make a conscious effort to find our own niche in life. We must build sufficient self-confidence and self-reliance to weather life's storms and to ward off assaults to our self-esteem.

Obviously, it is impossible to go through life without some negative experiences—experiences that can create self-doubts, and put questions in our minds about our abilities and sense of self-worth. These kinds of life circumstances can contribute to a negative self-image and low self-esteem if we let them. Blows to our self-respect and self-esteem can heal more slowly than do bodily injuries and can leave scars that are even more lasting. It is through the building of a more positive self-image and self-esteem that we can meet the many challenges of life and fulfill our basic needs of self-worth, self-acceptance, and personal happiness. We can conquer the enemy of a negative self-image and low self-esteem by achieving our potential self—by becoming what we can become.

GROWTH AND CHANGE ARE A LIFE LONG PROCESS

"We always contain within ourselves the possibility of change"

--Nathaniel Branden

Our self-image is not static or fixed and is always subject to change. In the development of a positive self-image and self-esteem, we must maintain a self-directed initiative. Through self-fulfilling activity, through working to achieve our self-selected values and goals, we can acquire genuine and authentic self-esteem.

Overnight self-image changes are extremely rare. We may, on occasion, experience sudden flashes of insight that promote change; but most changes in our self-concept are gradual and take time. Our self-image is a product of learning. It is learned throughout our entire life and should never be considered a completed fact. Our self-image is subject to development and change as long as we live. This is the most exciting and optimistic fact about self-image—knowing that self-image growth and self-esteem enhancement are always possible at any age no matter what our past experiences have been or how old we become.

Human growth is the result of personal action and effort. In the search for self-esteem, we must continue to have confidence in our ability to change and grow as a person. We must have hope for the future in order to have the courage to set new life goals leading to the enhancement of a more positive identity and self-esteem. Personal growth and self-realization mean that our attitudes, needs, values, and goals all change with age, new experiences, and increased self-knowledge. People's image of self can be continually modified to match their new standards, values, goals, personal expectations, and achievements. As people acquire genuine appreciation and regard for their own human dignity and worth as a person, they will find increasing hope for a fuller and richer life. Arthur Combs provides an excellent summary of the value of having a positive self-image when he writes:

> "Having a positive view of self is much like having money in the bank. It provides the kind of security that permits the owner freedom he could not have otherwise. With a positive view of self, one can risk taking chances; one does not have to be afraid of what is new and different. A sturdy ship can venture further from port. Just so, an adequate person can launch himself without fear into the new, the untried, and the unknown."

The second part of this book provides a systems approach to building a positive self-image and self-esteem. The activities and exercises found in the next section have been tried by many hundreds of people with very favorable results. The systems approach to self-actualization and human growth provides a valuable and useful tool for living a more satisfying, productive, and fulfilling life.

The following flow-chart depicts what the systems approach to building self-esteem looks like. (See next page).

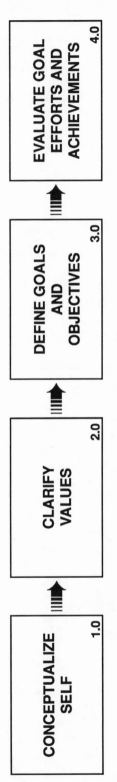

CONCEPTUALIZE
SELF
1.0

CLARIFY
VALUES
2.0

DEFINE GOALS
AND
OBJECTIVES
3.0

EVALUATE GOAL
EFFORTS AND
ACHIEVEMENTS
4.0

The system flow chart is provided as a visual guide to the self-esteem building process. Each one of the four system functions depicted in the flow chart builds on the other, thereby providing a logical and orderly process for goal-directed efforts and achievements.

PART TWO

A systems approach to achieving human potential and building self-esteem.

INTRODUCTION
PART TWO

The primary purpose of the first part of this book has been to acquaint you with a working knowledge of self-image theory and to provide information regarding the role that self-image and self-esteem play in everyday life. The purpose of this section of the book is to provide you with information and guidance in actively applying self-image theory in your own search for self-esteem.

The program for building self-esteem uses a system framework made up of four functions designed to actualize human potential and personal growth. The system model uses basic principles of organization and looks at all human beings in terms of systematic growth and development. A premise of the program is that all human beings have one central need in life, which is to achieve human potentialities. The human being is both an organic and functional system with the potential for human growth and change. The four system functions are identified as follows:

1. Conceptualize self
2. Clarify values
3. Define goals and objectives
4. Evaluate goal efforts and achievements

Each of these functions is described in detail in the following writing. A self-image inventory, participant tracking forms, and a number of exercises (which can be used as individual activities or for group processing) are also available. By using this material, you will be able to document a personal inventory of potentials and limitations, clarify personal values, translate potentials and values into goals and objectives, and evaluate personal goal efforts and achievements.

Though the material found in this book may be considered a self-help resource, it is not intended to be a form of mental health treatment or a substitute for psychotherapy. The exercises provided in this section of the book are designed to assist participants in the self-actualization process and are not intended to deal with past psychic wounds or emotional problems. The focus of the exercises should be primarily on present and future growth issues. The exercises are designed to provide the necessary awareness and information for the completion of the participant tracking forms found at the end of the exercises. Completion of these tracking forms provides valuable insight and information that makes personal growth and change attainable. Also allowing for monitoring overall program accomplishments and outcomes, the tracking forms are designed to provide and document personalized information needed for self-determined goal action and achievement.

SELF-IMAGE (SI)
INVENTORY

Prior to working on the following exercises for Conceptualize Self, Clarify Values, Define Goals and Objectives, and Evaluate Goal Efforts and Achievements, you are asked to complete the Self-Image (SI) Inventory (see next page). The SI Inventory is an instrument that can be used for examining different aspects of self-image and self-esteem. It is.important to remember, however, that self-image is a nebulous factor, lacking specific boundaries or limits, and cannot be measured on any absolute numerical scale. The SI Inventory should be viewed as a subjective self-image indicator rather than an absolute self-image trait assessment.

Our sense of personal adequacy cannot, of course, be measured on any absolute scale. We feel confident about some things, shaky about others. The SI Inventory is designed to help describe how people think and feel about themselves. This Self-Image Inventory is an indication of your self-esteem, your self-perception related to others, and your satisfaction with your role in life.

There are no right or wrong answers, and you are encouraged to respond to each statement as honestly as you can. Circle the letter that you feel best fits you. Complete the Inventory and score according to the number scale at the end.

1. In terms of attractiveness, I am:
    a. very attractive
    b. fairly attractive
    c. average
    d. passing
    e. unattractive

2. My personality is:
    a. very interesting
    b. fairly interesting
    c. average
    d. passing
    e. dull

3. I have:
    a. much confidence in myself
    b. enough confidence in myself
    c. average confidence in myself
    d. little confidence in myself
    e. no confidence in myself

4. I think that I get along with others:
    a. extremely well
    b. fairly well
    c. well enough
    d. not very well
    e. very poorly

5. When competing with others, I feel:
    a. I will usually win
    b. I have a good chance to win
    c. I will win sometimes
    d. I will usually not win
    e. I will probably never win

6. I dress:
   a. very well
   b. fairly well
   c. average
   d. don't care
   e. sloppy

7. When I walk into a room, I make:
   a. good impression
   b. fair impression
   c. average impression
   d. no impression
   e. dull impression

8. I accept personal compliments with:
   a. no embarrassment
   b. little embarrassment
   c. occasional embarrassment
   d. frequent embarrassment
   e. constant embarrassment

9. I feel confident that I will succeed in the future:
   a. all of the time
   b. most of the time
   c. some of the time
   d. hardly ever
   e. none of the time

10. In terms of maturity, I am:
    a. very mature
    b. fairly mature
    c. average
    d. below average
    e. immature

11. When among strangers, I feel:
    a. very comfortable
    b. fairly comfortable
    c. the same as usual
    d. uncomfortable
    e. extremely uncomfortable

12. I feel warm and happy toward myself:
    a. all of the time
    b. most of the time
    c. some of the time
    d. hardly ever
    e. none of the time

13. If I could make myself over, I would be:
    a. exactly as I am
    b. about the same
    c. slightly changed
    d. greatly changed
    e. another person

14. I experience enjoyment and zest for living:
    a. all of the time
    b. most of the time
    c. some of the time
    d. hardly ever
    e. none of the time

15. I admit my mistakes, shortcomings, and defeats:
    a. all of the time
    b. most of the time
    c. occasionally
    d. hardly ever
    e. none of the time

16. I usually feel inferior to others:
    a. none of the time
    b. hardly ever
    c. occasionally
    d. most of the time
    e. all of the time

17. I feel I am in control of my life:
    a. all of the time
    b. most of the time
    c. some of the time
    d. very little of the time
    e. none of the time

18. I have an intense need for recognition and approval:
    a. none of the time
    b. hardly ever
    c. occasionally
    d. most of the time
    e. all of the time

19. I try to live by my own values, beliefs, and convictions:
    a. all of the time
    b. most of the time
    c. some of the time
    d. very little of the time
    e. none of the time

20. I am able to solve my personal problems:
    a. all of the time
    b. most of the time
    c. some of the time
    d. very little of the time
    e. none of the time

21. I avoid new goal endeavors because of fear of mistakes or failures:
    a. none of the time
    b. very little of the time
    c. some of the time
    d. most of the time
    e. all of the time

22. I believe that I am achieving my human potential:
    a. all of the time
    b. most of the time
    c. some of the time
    d. very little of the time
    e. none of the time

* Score each question according to these values:a = +2; b = +1; c = 0; d = -1; e = -2. Then total plus and minus points. Subtract to get your score.

** A score of +35 to +15 indicates a positive self-image. A score of +14 to +O indicates an acceptable self-image. A score of -1 to -14 indicates a negative self-image. A score of -15 to -35 suggests significant self-rejection and feelings of inadequacy. A score of -36 to -44 indicates complete rejection of self. (Note: A score of +36 to +44 might indicate a rather inflated self-concept, perhaps as unrealistic as the opposite end of the scale.)

*** The SI Inventory is not intended to be used as a diagnostic test, but represents an inventory for self-awareness and exploration. It provides an instrument for examining different aspects of self-image, and can provide a reference point for self-image insight and change.

CONCEPTUALIZE SELF
(1.0)

As a former vocational guidance counselor, I am sensitive to the importance of knowing our potentials, limitations, aptitudes, and natural inclinations. I have seen many students who decided to attend college or a vocational school who had no idea of their area of concentration. As a late academic bloomer myself (beginning my college studies in my early 30s), I began my college experience with little or no idea of what major field of study would best suit my interests, aptitudes, and abilities. To be successful in the achievement of future goals, it is helpful to know as much as we can about ourselves and the world we live in. We must be aware of our capabilities as well as our human limitations. Personal strength acknowledgement is particularly important in successfully tapping potentials leading to human growth and a more positive self-image.

The self-image inventory that you just took was designed to help you to better understand yourself and assist you in better utilizing your unique potentials leading to greater human growth and personal development. The self-image inventory can help you list the traits you value in yourself and the skills you are most good at. The inventory can also reflect these characteristics that you see as personal liabilities or limitations. Knowing both your human potentials and limitations can help you make good choices and assist you in opening up new life opportunities. Almost all counselors would agree that the ability to know one's self is a basic requirement of good mental stability and personal adjustment. The Greek philosopher Socrates left us with sound words of wisdom, "Know thyself, know your strengths and your weaknesses, your potentials and limitations; take stock of yourself."

An accurate awareness of self can be a true asset in allowing us to determine our real needs, values, and life goals. Authentic self-knowledge is essential for the acquisition of a positive self-image and self esteem. We must think about our potentials and limitations if we are to experience personal growth and self-actualization. Truly knowing oneself leads to a greater sense of control over present and future life outcomes. People who know themselves can make decisions about what they want out of life—they know what they can and cannot realistically achieve.

The main purpose of the Conceptualize Self exercises is to provide you an opportunity to look at yourself in terms of the people and experiences that have helped form and shape your life and personal identity. In this process of self-discovery, emphasis should be placed on discovering the "potential self." The following exercises are designed to help you explore some of the life situations and experiences that have helped shape the way you think and feel about yourself today—your self-image. Change begins by being consciously aware of our true selves.

Upon completing the following exercises, you are asked to use the information obtained from these activities to complete the tracking forms found at the end of each function. The tracking forms become a very important information resource and can serve as a personal journal of your journey through the self-esteem enhancement process.

SELF-IMAGE SOURCES
EXERCISE (1.1)

Our self-image begins to develop in the formative years. Our immediate family is the first primary group giving us information regarding the kind of person we believe ourselves to be. School is another early source contributing to self-image development.

1. Recall your parents or surrogate (substitute parents) and briefly describe the ways in which you believe they affected your self-image. Include sibling influences if you had them.

_____

_____

_____

_____

_____

2. Recall your school experiences (up through high school) and briefly describe what effect school mates and teachers had on your self-image.

_____

_____

_____

_____

_____

POSITIVE AND NEGATIVE
EXPERIENCE EXERCISE (1.2)

Think back to some of your earlier years' experiences. Try to think of some of the very nicest experiences as well as some of your more negative experiences.

1. Recall one experience or event in your life that caused you to feel good about yourself. Briefly describe this experience or event and how it made you feel about yourself at the time.

_____

_____

_____

_____

_____

_____

2. Recall one experience or event in your life that caused you to feel badly about yourself. Briefly describe this experience or event and how it made you feel about yourself at the time.

_____

_____

_____

_____

_____

_____

CHILDHOOD LABELS
EXERCISE (1.3)

Early in life a child may be assigned a label, either positive or negative, which can influence self-image development. Following is a list of some common childhood labels. See if any of the labels apply to you. If not, think of other labels that you may have acquired from home or school.

Smart	Homely	Reliable
Dumb	Ambitious	Mischievous
Responsible	Lazy	Studious
Irresponsible	Funny	Indifferent
Strong	Serious	Popular
Weak	Generous	Shy
Athletic	Selfish	Cooperative
Clumsy	Honest	Uncooperative
Nice	Devious	Talkative
Spoiled	Talented	Quiet
Cute	Slow	Other

After identifying childhood labels from this list or from others you have thought of, respond to the following questions:

1. Did the label seem appropriate or accurate to you at the time?

2. Did you have more positive or more negative labels?

3. Do you feel that this label is still a part of your overall self-image?

PERSONALITY TRAIT
EXERCISE (1.4)

Our personality, like our self-image, begins to form in the developmental years. Personality includes all of the traits which tend to influence or make up our behavior. In the spaces below, try to list at least 15 personality traits that you like to see in others. Examples of desirable traits are friendly, kind, forgiving, tolerant, cooperative, etc.

1. List traits:

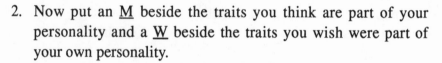

2. Now put an __M__ beside the traits you think are part of your personality and a __W__ beside the traits you wish were part of your own personality.

3. If you identified one or more of these traits that you think are not part of your personality but might wish them to be, what would you need to do to make them part of your personality?

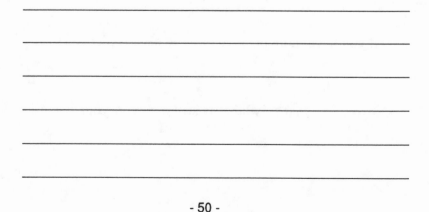

TURNING POINTS
EXERCISE (1.5)

Our self-image can be influenced by significant turning points in our lives. Think back to some turning point in your life, i.e., graduating from school, joining the service, getting married or divorced, taking a new job, retiring, etc. Then respond to the following statements or questions:

1. Identify and describe the turning point experience.

    _____

    _____

    _____

2. Did this turning point contribute in any way to your self-image?

    _____

    _____

    _____

3. Was this turning point a positive or negative experience for you?

    _____

    _____

    _____

4. Did the turning point help you grow as a person? If so, how?

    _____

    _____

    _____

SOCIAL APPROVAL
EXERCISE (1.6)

Everyone has a need for approval and acceptance. Gaining approval from significant others can often make us feel good about ourselves while being rejected or neglected can make us feel that we are worthless and that we are a nobody. Identify one person in your life, e.g., father, mother, teacher, employer, spouse, etc., whose approval was most important and think about how you felt in getting or not getting this person's approval.

Respond to the following questions:

1. Did *getting* this person's approval in any way affect the way you now think or feel about yourself as a person?

_____

_____

_____

_____

_____

2. Did *not getting* this person's approval in any way affect the way you now think or feel about yourself as a person?

_____

_____

_____

_____

_____

NEGATIVE SELF-TALK
EXERCISE (1.7)

Self-image traits are often influenced and established by self-talk, i.e., what we tell ourselves about ourselves in certain situations. Self-talk may be either negative or positive. We can experience a sense of self-rejection and self-doubt through negative self-talk.

1. Think of a situation where you made a mistake or experienced personal failure.

   _____

   _____

2. Recall and describe what negative self-talk you may have used that made you feel guilty or bad about yourself because of the mistake or failure.

   _____

   _____

3. Without being defensive or making excuses, what positive things could you have said about the mistake or failure that could have helped you think and feel better about yourself.

   _____

   _____

4. Can you see the specific mistake or personal failure as a positive learning experience that could help you avoid this or similar mistakes and failures in the future?

   _____

   _____

5. Can you think of some other situations in which you could have changed negative self-talk to positive self-talk?

   _____

   _____

SELF-IDEAL
EXERCISE (1.8)

The self-ideal, in contrast to how we see ourselves, is the way we would like to be. It consists of our hopes and aspirations for ourselves—the kind of person we wish to be or would like to become. Others whom we respect, admire, or see as positive role models can influence our self-ideal. Try and identify three people (living or dead) who have influenced your own self-ideal.

Following are three people who have been positive role models in your life:

1. _____

   Why? _____

   _____

   _____

2. _____

   Why? _____

   _____

   _____

3. _____

   Why? _____

   _____

   _____

SELF-IMAGE PROJECTION
EXERCISE (1.9)

All people project a self-image to others that may or may not be consistent with how they really see themselves. Write answers to the following:

1. Write down three words or adjectives that best describe you as a person.

   _____

   _____

   _____

2. Now write down three words or adjectives that you would like others to use in describing you as a person:

   _____

   _____

   _____

3. In what way, if any, would you like to improve your projected image?

   _____

   _____

   _____

   _____

   _____

UNIQUE TALENTS
EXERCISE (1.10)

Our personal characteristics, abilities, and talents make us unique. Each one of us has unique potentials, aptitudes, and natural inclinations making us different from other people we know. Your unique talents are the guidelines for developing your own human potentials and enhancing self-esteem.

List the unique talents you feel you have in any of the following areas:

Occupational Talents _____

_____

Educational Talents _____

_____

Social Talents _____

_____

Physical Talents _____

_____

Mental Talents _____

_____

Musical Talents _____

_____

Artistic Talents _____

_____

Avocational Talents _____

_____

Athletic Talents _____

_____

CONCEPTUALIZE SELF TRACKING FORM (1.0)

Potentials and Limitations Inventory

1. The following are what I see as my basic potentials or personal assets:

   _____

   _____

   _____

2. The following are what I see as my basic limitations or personal liabilities:

   _____

   _____

   _____

3. I could take better advantage of my potentials by:

   _____

   _____

   _____

4. I could overcome some of my limitations by:

   _____

   _____

   _____

CONCEPTUALIZE SELF
TRACKING FORM—NOTES

CLARIFY VALUES
(2.0)

After conceptualizing self, the next function is to clarify personal values. The purpose of this function is to assist you in better knowing your values and to resolve possible value conflicts that may be going on in your life. If you know what is most important to you in your life, then you know your values. Values can be tangible or intangible. You may value such entities as yourself, another person, a relationship, your family, an education, a job, personal growth, security, achievement, pleasure, material goods, money, religion, and so on. Knowing your values is important because you live by them and work for them.

Self-realization requires that all human beings seek some system of values to which they can commit themselves. Belief in a value system serves as a guide to our personal decisions, actions, and behavior. Personal growth requires that we adopt a value system that can lead to rational planning and thoughtful action. It is through our value system that we are able to achieve personal goals. Translating our values into specific and meaningful goals is essential for personal growth and self-actualization.

We are each responsible for choosing our own values that guide our actions and determine our goals. It is quite possible that with the passing of time we will change some of our values. In values clarification, it is assumed that you have the freedom to select your own values after thoughtful consideration of both the good and bad consequences. It is important to remember that we can always choose our own values, but we cannot always choose the consequences of these value choices.

You will regard certain of your values as more important to you than others. It is, therefore, important that you learn how to rank or prioritize your values in order to make responsible and informed decisions. Resolving value conflicts is a part of everyday life for most of us. Being able to decide which value is most important is necessary in the value conflict resolution process.

Our self-selected values are vital to the development of a unifying philosophy of life. Our values can provide a healthy outlook for the future and become the foundation for our hopes, aspirations, and dreams. Values provide the cornerstone of life and give us our very purpose for living. Human growth may be defined as self-change in a valued direction.

The following exercises are designed to help you to clarify your own values. If you aren't sure of your present values, then these exercises will help you to see them more clearly. Use the information from the values clarification exercise to assist you in completing the values clarification tracking form.

VALUE RANKING
EXERCISE (2.1)

You will regard certain of your values as more important to you than others. Rank the following nine values from the most important to the least important. Place the number <u>one</u> by the most important value, the number <u>two</u> by the second most important value and so on through number <u>nine</u>, the least important value.

_____   Money

_____   Love (affection, acceptance)

_____   Self-esteem

_____   Health (Physical and Mental)

_____   Education (Knowledge)

_____   Work (Job Satisfaction)

_____   Leisure

_____   Security

_____   Family

VALUE SOURCES
EXERCISE (2.2)

Values are learned and may be acquired from many sources such as family, friends, teachers, clergy, role models, advertising media, etc. Read and then respond to the following questions or statements:

1. Review your value system and select two values that are most important to you.

   _____

   _____

2. How do you think you acquired these values?

   _____

   _____

3. Were these values freely chosen by you?

   _____

   _____

4. Were they chosen from alternatives?

   _____

   _____

5. Do you think your present behavior or actions are consistent with these values? If not, what could you do to bring your behavior or actions more in line with your values?

   _____

   _____

PHILOSOPHY OF LIFE
EXERCISE (2.3)

Philosophy is defined as a system of values by which one lives. Fill out the following personal philosophy questionnaire:

1. What do you want out of life?

    _____

    _____

    _____

2. What would it be like to live the life you want to live?

    _____

    _____

    _____

3. What kind of person do you want to be?

    _____

    _____

    _____

4. What contributions would you like to make during your life?

    _____

    _____

    _____

5. How can you translate your philosophy of life into meaningful and achievable goals, i.e., how can you live your philosophy?

    _____

    _____

    _____

VALUES CLARIFICATION
EXERCISE (2.4)

Review the following list of values and check 10 that are most applicable to your own value system. Go back over the ones you checked to see which ones, if any, are not being fulfilled. What do you think you could do to better fulfill the values not presently being realized?

_____ Sociability	_____ Freedom
_____ Companionship	_____ Work
_____ Knowledge	_____ Pleasure
_____ Independence	_____ Health
_____ Security	_____ Cooperation
_____ Love	_____ Decency
_____ Happiness	_____ Personal Appearance
_____ Achievement	_____ Self-Control
_____ Ambition	_____ Self-Responsibility
_____ Assertiveness	_____ Self-Acceptance
_____ Honesty	_____ Self-Confidence
_____ Cheerfulness	_____ Self-Trust
_____ Prosperity	_____ Self-Respect
_____ Leisure	_____ Self-Esteem

VALUE CONFLICT
EXERCISE (2.5)

At times, your values may be in conflict. When two or more values are being held at the same level of importance, you may experience value conflicts. You must, therefore, decide which value is most important to you in order to resolve the conflict. Respond to the following value conflict situations:

1. You value justice and honesty. You also value money. What would you do if you found a wallet containing an ID and $100 in cash?

    _____

    _____

2. You value yourself. You also value your friends. How far would you go to do something to deprive yourself to please your friends?

    _____

    _____

3. You value your health and safety. You also value fun. To what extent would you abuse your body, or risk danger in order to have a good time?

    _____

    _____

4. You value competition. You also value cooperation. To what degree would you use competition in pursuing your own interests and concerns over cooperation with others?

    _____

    _____

5. You value your own ideas and opinions. You also value the ideas and opinions of others. How firmly would you stand on your own opinions and ideas over the opinions and ideas of others?

    _____

    _____

VALUE AWARENESS
EXERCISE (2.6)

This exercise is designed to help you see what your values are now. If you're not sure of your values, this process may help you to see them more clearly or to decide what you want your values to be.

Identify two objects that are now in your possession, e.g., wedding ring, picture of spouse or loved one, credit card, car or house keys, etc. Now think about how these two things are seen as a value in your own life and then respond to the following questions?

1. Is it necessary to have personal values to live by?

    _____

    _____

2. Are you presently living your values?

    _____

    _____

3. Do you feel your values are fulfilling your personal needs and purpose in life?

    _____

    _____

4. Are you experiencing any personal value conflicts in your life? If so, what are they?

    _____

    _____

VALUE CHOICE
EXERCISE (2.7)

You are asked to make an inventory of eight material possessions most valued. The list can include large or small items—a house, a car, a TV, a stereo, a piece of jewelry, etc. They need not be your possessions with the highest monetary worth.

Eight Material Possessions You Value Most

_____	_____
_____	_____
_____	_____
_____	_____

1. Now imagine that, owing to certain circumstances, you can keep only four of these possessions. Which four would you choose and why?

   _____

   _____

2. As you narrowed your choice from eight to four, what did you have to consider?

   _____

   _____

3. What conflicts of values, if any, did you encounter in making each choice?

   _____

   _____

4. Did you have to consider the values of others, i.e., spouse, child, friend, etc., in making your choice?

   _____

   _____

VALUE MODIFICATION
EXERCISE (2.7)

Many of your values will remain stable throughout your life while others will change. Many of your values were acquired early in life and some may no longer meet your needs. You may, therefore, need to modify or change parts of your value system.

1. You are asked to identify one personal value that you might like to change.

   _____

   _____

2. How do you think you acquired this particular value? e.g., from family, school, church, peers, etc.?

   _____

   _____

3. In what way does this value affect your present attitudes and life situation?

   _____

   _____

4. What might be a viable alternative value or viewpoint?

   _____

   _____

5. How might incorporating the modified or alternative value into your overall life philosophy be beneficial to you and/ or others?

   _____

   _____

VALUES AND WORK
EXERCISE (2.9)

Knowing your values is important because you live by them and work for them. Your values hold the key to your work motivation and job satisfaction.

1. What is the thing that you like most about your present work?

_____

_____

_____

2. What is the thing that you dislike most about your present work?

_____

_____

_____

3. Are you doing the kind of work you want to be doing? Do you value your work or would you rather be doing something else?

_____

_____

_____

4. Is there anything you could do to get more job satisfaction? If so, what is it?

_____

_____

_____

VALUES AND GOAL RELATIONSHIP EXERCISE (2.10)

Growing toward a fully functioning and self-actualized individual requires the clarification of personal values and the translation of values into goals and objectives. Failing to achieve our values can result in diminished self-esteem while realizing our values through goal accomplishments can enhance self-esteem. You are asked to identify and translate one personal unfulfilled value to a goal activity.

1. Your unfulfilled value is: (A value is defined as what you believe to be of importance and worth to you.)

   _____

   _____

2. Your value realization goal is: (A goal is defined as a value toward which an endeavor is directed.)

   _____

   _____

3. After identifying a value and goal, you are asked to respond to the following questions:

   Do you really want the goal?

   Is the goal right according to your value system?

   Will you be a more fulfilled person when you accomplish the goal?

   Will accomplishing the goal have any benefit to others?

   Is your goal legally, morally, and socially acceptable?

   Will you have to compromise any of your values in achieving this goal?

VALUES CLARIFICATION TRACKING FORM (2.0)

Your values hold the key to your personal life style and are the guiding factors to your future goals. Your values influence your decisions and behavior and give meaning and purpose to your present and future life.

Write a brief value statement in each of the three following areas:

1. Values I hold about myself are, e.g., self-worth values such as honesty or integrity:

    _____

    _____

    _____

2. Values I hold about my present life are, e.g., job, family, material possessions:

    _____

    _____

    _____

3. Values I hold about my future life are, e.g., things you want to do, achieve, experience, or become:

    _____

    _____

    _____

VALUES CLARIFICATION
TRACKING FORM—NOTES

DEFINE GOALS AND OBJECTIVES (3.0)

After having completed the first two steps of self-discovery and values clarification, it is now time to put this information into personal action. It is now time to translate your potentials and values into self-selected goals and objectives. Goal setting is an action and knowing who you are and what you want is essential for goal identification and goal accomplishment.

For many of us, goals are things we want to achieve, experience, or accomplish that are way off in the future. Sometimes we look at our future goals as if we were going to live forever. It is important to realize that your personal goals provide a way for you to make a positive difference in your life right now. When you set and achieve a goal, you are increasing your sense of self-worth, self-confidence, self-initiative, and self-determination. Goal setting and achievement allow you the freedom to take charge of your own life. Goal setting is something you can do to better yourself. Goals allow you to work towards a new destination in human growth and to create your own future.

It is important to understand the relationship between goals and objectives while also being able to distinguish between the different meanings of these two terms. A goal may be defined in more general terms than an objective. A goal is a statement of what one wishes to accomplish, acquire or achieve. The goal of becoming a more happy person is an example of a common goal. An objective, on the other hand, is a specific action or activity one must take in order to achieve the goal. An objective is a statement of what one must do in order to make the goal an accomplished reality. Objectives need to be stated as behavioral objectives. That is, an objective must be stated in a specific way that will allow it to become measurable.

For instance, in the example of the goal of happiness, one must identify the specific actions one needs to take in achieving happiness. Perhaps the loss of 10 pounds of body weight within the next month would result in personal gratification and happiness. This loss of 10 pounds within a month becomes the objective since this accomplishment is clearly specific and easily measurable. All one needs to do in this case is to get on the scale at the beginning of the designated time period and again at the end, to see if the weight loss goal has been met.

Another way to distinguish between goals and objectives is to consider the well-known ancient Chinese proverb, "A journey of a thousand miles begins with a single step." The thousand mile journey is the general goal while the first step, which is necessary measurable action one must take to reach the goal, may be viewed as a specific objective.

Though it is true that some goals may not be as easy to translate into behavioral objectives as the two examples just given, all goals need to be placed within observable, measurable time boundaries. Some other related criteria should also be considered regarding the establishment of goals and objectives which are listed as follows:

SPECIFIC GOALS

Goals need to be stated in specific terms. Goals such as "I'm going to become a happier person" are not sufficient because they are too general. General goals tend to be vague and nebulous. In order to identify steps in achieving goals, the goals must be defined and stated in more specific terms. Failure to achieve goals is often due to the failure to identify specific objectives.

REALISTIC GOALS

Goals must be in keeping with our potentials and limitations. Setting goals too high invites failure while setting goals too low can result in settling for second best. Goals must be realistic in keeping with individual potentials and resources, and should be aimed at the elimination of self-defeating behaviors.

MEANINGFUL GOALS

A goal that is not considered valuable or one that has no practical application to the individual will be viewed as meaningless and not worthy of personal effort. Individuals must first clarify values before they can translate values to goals and objectives. Goals become a way of allowing people to live their values.

MEASURABLE GOALS

Goals need to be measurable. This not only helps to get started, but also provides the opportunity to check goal progress toward goal achievement. Putting goals into time boundaries can also reduce the chance for goal procrastination.

PLAN OF ACTION

"Failing to plan is planning to fail." A well thought out plan of action is usually necessary in order to become sufficiently motivated toward goal achievement. Identifying a clear path to a desired goal can increase efforts in attaining the goal. Planning keeps people oriented toward the future and allows them to gauge both short- and long-term goal efforts and accomplishments.

GOAL COMMITMENT

The relationship between values and goal commitment is obvious. The more value placed on the goal, the more commitment people are likely to make toward it. A half-hearted goal commitment will result in a half-hearted effort. Commitment is best achieved through self-selected and nonimposed goals. Commitment to working on goals that have not been voluntarily chosen will be a weak commitment at best.

The following exercises are provided to assist you in identifying your goals and objectives which you are to document on the Define Goals and Objectives Tracking Form.

PERSONAL GOAL ACHIEVEMENT EXERCISE (3.1)

Everyone has experienced goal achievement in life. When you set and achieve a goal, you are doing something positive for yourself. Achieving your goal gives you feelings of self-confidence, self-reliance, and self-worth. Think of one personal goal achievement that made you feel good about yourself and then respond to the following questions:

1. What were your feelings about the goal achievement experience at the time?

_____

_____

_____

2. Are you having enough goal achievement experiences in your life today?

_____

_____

_____

3. What goal achievement would you most like to experience next in your life?

_____

_____

_____

GOAL AWARENESS
EXERCISE (3.2)

Goal setting and achievement allow you to take charge of your own life and create your own future. Respond to the following goal setting and achievement questions:

1. Are you satisfied enough with your present life that you feel no further goals are necessary? If not, what personal goals do you consider to be of ultimate importance in your life?

    _____

    _____

    _____

2. Do you feel you have the necessary potentials, motivation, and resources to achieve these goals?

    _____

    _____

    _____

3. Are achieving these goals worth the effort, time, and energy required by you?

    _____

    _____

    _____

4. How would you feel about yourself if and when you achieve these goals?

    _____

    _____

    _____

GOAL COMMITMENT
EXERCISE (3.3)

Goal setting is either a mental or physical action and can involve something you want to do or to stop doing. List several activities you would like to do but have not done yet. Then list several activities you are doing that you would like to stop doing.

1. Activities I want to do:

   _____

   _____

   _____

   _____

2. Activities I want to stop doing:

   _____

   _____

   _____

   _____

Pick one *to do* and one *not to do* activity as a personal goal and make a commitment to yourself to make an effort to achieve goals. List some specific steps you need to take to achieve each goal.

GOAL IDENTIFICATION
EXERCISE (3.4)

For many people, goals are pushed off into the future; but your personal goals can provide a way for you to make a positive difference in your life right now. Think of at least two goals that could make you feel better about yourself:

Now respond to the following two questions:

1. Do you see any reason why you cannot start working on these goals right away? If so, what are they?

_____

_____

_____

_____

2. What obstacles do you see to achieving these goals and what resources or abilities do you have to overcome the obstacles?

_____

_____

_____

_____

PERSONAL GOALS AND
OBJECTIVES EXERCISE (3.5)

By changing the way we act, we can often change the way we think and feel about ourselves. Some negative self-perceptions can readily be changed through minor shifts in behavior.

1. You are asked to identify one perception of yourself that you would like to change. For example, "I think of myself as being inconsiderate of others. I would like to change that."

_____

_____

_____

2. You are now asked to think of some possible ways of changing the self-perception. Make a plan to change the way you think of yourself so that you will no longer think of self as ..., e.g., inconsiderate of others, as in the preceding example.

_____

_____

_____

3. You are now asked to describe a plan of action you wish to take in modifying this behavior. Briefly state your plan of action, which should include consideration of who, what, where, when, and how.

_____

_____

_____

GOAL SETTING
EXERCISE (3.6)

Your life is yours to live. Achieving life goals can bring you the greatest feelings of personal satisfaction and self-regard. Answer the following life goal setting and achievement questions:

1. If you learned today that you would die in six months, how would you really want to live until then? What kinds of things would you want to do?

   _____

   _____

   _____

2. What are the most satisfying ways you currently spend your time?

   _____

   _____

   _____

3. How would you like to spend the next four years of your life?

   _____

   _____

   _____

4. What would you really like to achieve in your life? What would you like to become?

   _____

   _____

   _____

5. What goal or goals could you set to enhance your quality of life?

   _____

   _____

   _____

LONG- AND SHORT-RANGE
GOAL EXERCISE (3.7)

Goal setting involves both long-range and short-range goals. Goal planning should provide a systematic process for goal effort and goal attainment. Goal planning discourages procrastination and allows for a greater utilization of human potential. Following is a list of some common goal areas in life that lend themselves to goal setting. You are asked to identify a long- and short-range goal in one of the following or other selected life area:

1. Career Long-Range Goal: _____

    Career Short-Range Goal: _____

2. Financial Long-Range Goal: _____

    Financial Short-Range Goal: _____

3. Family Long-Range Goal: _____

    Family Short-Range Goal: _____

4. Education Long-Range Goal: _____

    Education Short-Range Goal: _____

5. Health Long-Range Goal: _____

    Health Short-Range Goal: _____

6. Leisure Long-Range Goal: _____

    Leisure Short-Range Goal: _____

7. Other Long-Range Goal: _____

    Other Short-Range Goal: _____

GOAL PRIORITY
EXERCISE (3.8)

Setting goals based on your values provides a chance to put your values
into action. It may become clear that, just like values, some goals are
more important to you than others. The following five questions can help
you to prioritize your goals?

1. Do you see yourself as a goal-setting and goal-achieving person?

    _____

    _____

    _____

2. What is your most important goal in life?

    _____

    _____

    _____

3. What is your most important goal priority next month?

    _____

    _____

    _____

4. Where do you want to be one year from now?

    _____

    _____

    _____

5. Where do you want to be five years from now?

    _____

    _____

    _____

GOAL ACTION
EXERCISE (3.9)

For personal goals to be achieved, a plan of action must be established. A written plan helps to visualize the goal outcomes. Having a goal plan can assist you to mobilize your own talents, abilities, and potentials for successful goal achievement.

1. Identify several personal life goals that you have already accomplished.

_____

_____

_____

2. Identify one or more goals yet to be accomplished. (It is recommended that no more than three goals be identified at any one time.)

_____

_____

_____

3. Identify specific steps needed to be taken in order to accomplish the goal or goals you wish to achieve. Briefly state your plan of action, which should include consideration of who, what, where, when, and how.

_____

_____

_____

PROBLEM-SOLVING AND GOAL-SETTING EXERCISE (3.10)

Problem solving and goal setting are often interrelated. As individuals, we try to solve problems and set goals almost every day of our lives. Usually there are alternative solutions to a problem. You are asked to identify a problem with which you are faced. State the problem and list as many alternative solutions as you can think of. (Also consider possible outcomes of each alternative.)

1. Your problem is: _____

    Alternative Solution: _____

    _____

    Possible Outcome: _____

    _____

    Alternative Solution: _____

    _____

    Possible Outcome: _____

    _____

    Alternative Solution: _____

    _____

    Possible Outcome: _____

    _____

2. You have chosen the following alternative: _____

    _____

    because: _____

    _____

DEFINE PERSONAL GOALS AND OBJECTIVES (3.0) TRACKING FORM

GOAL COMMITMENT

This establishes my personal goals that I am committed to achieving:

1. My goals are: (Briefly state goals as you understand them to be.)

   _____

   _____

   _____

2. My plan of accomplishing these goals is: (Briefly state your plan of action which should include who, what, where, when, and how.)

   _____

   _____

   _____

3. I plan to accomplish my goal by:

   Goal_____
   | | Day | Month | Year |

   Goal_____
   | | Day | Month | Year |

   Goal_____
   | | Day | Month | Year |

   Goal_____
   | | Day | Month | Year |

4. My checklist for goals include:

	YES	NO
Are goals specific?	____	____
Are goals realistic?	____	____
Are goals relevant?	____	____
Are goals measurable?	____	____

DEFINE PERSONAL GOALS AND OBJECTIVES TRACKING FORM—NOTES

EVALUATE GOAL EFFORTS AND ACHIEVEMENTS (4.0)

In giving much thought to the self-evaluation process of goal efforts, I came up with what I call the PHD acronym of goal sabotage. The P stands for Procrastination, the H for Habits, and the D for Dependencies. In this section, we will begin by looking at each one of these factors that can stifle our goal efforts.

PROCRASTINATION

Webster defines procrastination as follows: "To put off doing something until a future time, to postpone or delay endlessly." Procrastination involves specific goals or tasks that are considered important but which we fail to start. There are far too many possible causes for procrastination to begin to list them all here. I would, therefore, like to address one of the main factors contributing to procrastination which is low self-esteem. Low self-esteem fosters feelings of self-doubt and self-depreciation. Lacking self-confidence and self-reliance can lead to postponing activities that could result in defeat or failure. People very often procrastinate because they believe they may fail in the task. Procrastination can be a way of protecting oneself from the fear of making a mistake. Doubting one's own potentials and capabilities can cause one to postpone or put off activities or goals which surpass one's feelings of self-confidence, self-reliance, and self-esteem.

HABITS

Habits are actions or behaviors that one takes automatically or unconsciously through frequent repetition. It has been said that habits can be the best of servants or the worst of masters. We can have good habits that can eliminate the unnecessary expenditure of time and energy in our daily activities. Negative personal habits can, however, be a deterrent in the goal-effort accomplishment and achievement process. Some habits are helpful in that they may be effective timesavers while others may be most counterproductive. The breaking of negative or unwanted habits can be a hard and difficult process. Part of the function of goal-effort evaluation, then, is to consider personal habits that may stifle self-improvement or work against fulfillment of our human growth goals and objectives.

DEPENDENCIES

Dependency is a condition that can deprive people of their freedom to choose their own course of action leading toward personal growth and self-fulfillment. In goal setting, you are taking charge of your own life, not waiting for others to do so. Negative self-image people tend to believe they are unable to choose their own goals and look to others to set goals for them. Over-dependent people do not have a good sense of their own potentials and limitations, or of personal values underlying life goals and objectives. They tend to yield control of their lives to others, letting others dictate the actions they themselves could have taken. Excessive dependency can be a serious and crippling handicap in achieving our desired goals and objectives.

In the goal-effort evaluation process, it is important to remember that our goals may be blocked by our own internal factors such as procrastination, habits, and dependencies. If the goal block is coming from within ourselves, we must work to change our thoughts, feelings, and attitudes towards ourselves. Goal blocks, however, can also come from external factors such as other people or situations outside of ourselves over which we may have little or no control. It is most important, therefore, that we consider the possibility of these external goal blocks in our plan of action for goal achievement.

Self-evaluation of goal efforts must always include total self-acceptance. Total self-acceptance is absolutely essential for self-esteem. Failing to achieve our goals should never lead to self-rejection or self-downing. It is important that we always continue to accept ourselves as worthwhile and capable individuals with the necessary potential for human growth and change. Maintaining an attitude of self-respect and self-worth in the goal-effort evaluation process will provide the courage and tenacity to pursue goals regardless of obstacles, temporary setbacks, or difficult situations. The following exercises are provided to assist you in monitoring your goal efforts and achievements. Use the Goal Effort Tracking Form to monitor your goal efforts.

GOAL PROCRASTINATION EXERCISE (4.1)

Procrastination can have multiple causes. Most of us have many different reasons or excuses for putting off goal action. The following activity can provide insight regarding your own goal procrastination.

1. Identify a personal goal that you have failed to get started on:

   _____

   _____

   _____

2. What excuses or permission do you give yourself for not working on your goal?

   _____

   _____

   _____

3. What are your feelings about the goal?

   _____

   _____

   _____

4. What personal commitments and action steps can you make to overcome your goal procrastination?

   _____

   _____

   _____

HABIT AWARENESS
EXERCISE (4.2)

In evaluating goal efforts, it is important that we understand the nature of habits that can interfere with goal achievement. The following activity can help you identify those habit areas that may be interfering with your goal efforts.

1. Major Habits or Routines: Change Desired:

     Work _____

     Food _____

   Alcohol or Drugs _____

    Leisure Time _____

     Money _____

     Family _____

     Health _____

     Other _____

2. Questions:

Would a change in certain habits be beneficial to you?

_____

_____

What change in habits would make you feel better about yourself?

_____

_____

What change in habits would help you enjoy life more?

_____

_____

What change in habits would help you in your goal efforts?

_____

_____

PERSONAL DEPENDENCY
EXERCISE (4.3)

Excessive dependence on others or external sources can stifle our own goal efforts. We need to overcome childhood dependencies that stifle our own goal efforts and achievements. You are asked to identify someone or something on which you feel dependent and respond to the following three dependency questions. (If you feel you have no present dependencies, you can skip this exercise.)

1. When your dependency on this source is not satisfied, how do you feel?

2. Does this dependency in any way hinder your personal goal effort?

3. What could you do to overcome this dependency?

SELF-ACTUALIZATION
EXERCISE (4.4)

Self-actualization means to realize human potential through personal effort or action. All people have a need to work toward achieving their own potential, to develop talents and attain personal goals. Self-actualization through goal effort and action can help us to gain a sense of personal pride, self-worth, and self-esteem. Identify your most recent self-actualization experience and respond to the following three questions:

1. Did this self-actualization experience help you grow as a person? If so, how?

   _____

   _____

   _____

2. Did this self-actualization experience in any way enhance your feelings of self-esteem, self-confidence, and self-worth?

   _____

   _____

   _____

3. The value of self-actualization is the need to do what you are capable of doing—to achieve your potential in order to be fulfilled as a person. Can you identify other areas of self-actualization that could help you more effectively achieve your potential?

   _____

   _____

   _____

GOAL OBSTACLE
EXERCISE (4.5)

In our efforts to reach goals, we may experience certain obstacles that can hinder goal achievement. Sometimes the achievement of a goal can be blocked by *internal* factors or *external* factors. Internal factors may be such things as lack of self-confidence, lack of effort, or fear of failure. External factors could include other people or situations outside of ourselves. You are asked to list your goals and identify what internal or external obstacles may be hindering your goal achievement:

1. Goal: _____

   Goal Obstacles: _____

   _____

   What can be done to overcome these obstacles? _____

   _____

2. Goal: _____

   Goal Obstacles: _____

   _____

   What can be done to overcome these obstacles? _____

   _____

3. Goal: _____

   Goal Obstacles: _____

   What can be done to overcome these obstacles? _____

   _____

   _____

GOAL EFFORT
EXERCISE (4.6)

Being challenged with a new goal can be a richly rewarding experience providing we are able and willing to make the necessary goal effort. You are asked to identify a personally selected goal and then respond to the following goal effort statements or questions:

1. What is your selected specific goal?

   _____

   _____

2. What is happening regarding your goal effort?

   _____

   _____

3. What is not happening regarding your goal effort?

   _____

   _____

4. Do you need more goal effort motivation to accomplish your goal?

   _____

   _____

5. What are the possible causes of your lack of necessary goal effort?

   _____

   _____

6. What kind of a goal effort plan can you make to better increase your goal effort?

   _____

   _____

SELF-RESPONSIBILITY
EXERCISE (4.7)

Goal effort requires a sense of personal responsibility. You are asked to recall three positive life experiences and three negative life experiences. Write them down in the following spaces, and then put an X in front of those experiences resulting from personal responsibility and an O in front of those involving no personal responsibility:

1. _____ Positive Experience:

_____

_____

2. _____ Positive Experience:

_____

_____

3. _____ Positive Experience:

_____

_____

1. _____ Negative Experience:

_____

_____

2. _____ Negative Experience:

_____

_____

3. _____ Negative Experience:

_____

_____

SELF-IMAGE AND SELF-CONTROL EXERCISE (4.8)

Positive self-control is very important in maintaining a positive image of self and achieving personal goals. Oftentimes we may feel we are victims, or have little or no control over life circumstances. You are asked to consider and respond to the following questions:

1. Are there things happening to you in your present life that you feel you have no control over? If so, what are they?

_____

_____

2. Are you actively in charge of your own life or just a victim of life circumstances?

_____

_____

3. Are there things going on in your life that lie within your control, either through a change in your social or physical environment, or change in yourself?

_____

_____

4. What other things can you do to achieve your goals or to get more self-control over your life?

_____

_____

GOAL EFFORT
SUPPORT SYSTEM (4.9)

A major factor in goal accomplishment and achievement is the amount of social support available to us. Such a support system can provide encouragement and constructive feedback related to our goal efforts and achievement.

1. Take a moment to list the people who make up your support system:

    _____

    _____

    _____

2. How are they encouraging and supportive in your goal efforts?

    _____

    _____

    _____

3. Think of someone for whom you have the potential to be a supportive influence—what are some specific ways you support them in their goal efforts and achievement?

    _____

    _____

    _____

RESISTANCE TO CHANGE
EXERCISE (4.10)

Self-change can be a difficult task that is often met with some resistance. We need to identify forces working against change. A list of common factors that can stifle positive change follows. Carefully check the list to see if any of these factors apply to you:

_____ Unclear goals and objectives

_____ Fear of failure

_____ Fear of Success

_____ Lack of confidence in ability to change

_____ Satisfaction with status quo

_____ Lack of understanding about what changes are needed

_____ Failure in planning for change

_____ Inadequate rewards for change

_____ Failure of evaluating progress toward change

_____ Past experience with change

_____ Lack of effort to change

_____ Reaction of other people to change

GOAL EFFORT EVALUATION
TRACKING FORM (4.0)

WEEKLY SELF-EVALUATION CHECK LIST OF GOAL
EFFORTS WHICH BEGINS AS SOON AS PERSONAL GOALS
HAVE BEEN IDENTIFIED

MY GOALS	1	2	3	4	5	6	7	WEEK 8	9	10	11	12	13	14	15	16

MARK YOURSELF FOR YOUR WEEKLY GOAL EFFORT USING
THE FOLLOWING SCALE:
  O = No Effort   1 = Some Effort   2 = Good Effort   3 = Excellent Effort

GOAL EFFORT EVALUATION TRACKING FORM—NOTES

AFTERWORD

Almost monthly, a new crop of self-help books and motivational tapes become available. I do not question the efficacy of these books and tapes in creating intellectual insights, but my experience tells me that just reading books and listening to tapes will not by themselves enhance self-esteem. Self-awareness from books and tapes is usually quite transitory and very short-lived. For long lasting and continuous change to occur, self-awareness must be translated into personal action. We need more than just motivational cheerleading and self-affirmations to build self-esteem. We must also work to achieve our human potential. A positive inner view of our own self-worth is a product of self-realization and self-actualization—becoming what we can become.

Self-awareness is necessary for change but not sufficient. Change requires that individuals establish personal life goals that will allow them to translate awareness into action. The program described in this book is based on the premise that human beings are potentially in the state of becoming more than they are, or believe themselves to be, provided they have the self-awareness and intrinsic motivation to do so.

Human growth and self-esteem are both linked to the search of higher levels of self-actualization and self-fulfillment. The purpose of this book is to help you gain self-awareness, clarify values, set goals, and become more aware of how to overcome goal obstacles in your own quest for self-esteem. By overcoming your goal obstacles, you will be able to turn your stumbling blocks into stepping stones.

The writing of this book has been underway for a very long time and has evolved out of my conviction that a systematic approach to building self-esteem could be accomplished. I do not suggest that the program described in this book provides a miraculous solution to all human problems, but it has offered an approach which has proven successful in helping many people to start a new way of life and subsequently to feel better about themselves. I do not pretend to have found all the answers to the complex task of actualizing human potential and building self-esteem; but if this work continues to assist others in their quest for self-esteem, then my efforts have been richly rewarded.

BIBLIOGRAPHY

Allport, Gordon W. BECOMING. New Haven and London: Yale University Press, 1955.

Brande, Dorothea. WAKEUP AND LIVE. New York: Cornerstone Library, 1974.

Branden, Nathaniel. THE PSYCHOLOGY OF SELF-ESTEEM. New York: Bantam Books, 1969.

THE DISOWNED SELF. New York: Bantam Books, 1973.

HONORING THE SELF. New York: Bantam Books, 1984.

HOW TO RAISE YOUR SELF-ESTEEM. New York: Bantam Books, 1987.

Briggs, Dorothy C. YOUR CHILD'S SELF-ESTEEM. Garden City, NJ: Doubleday, 1970.

Canfield, Jack, and Wells, Harold C. 100 WAYS TO ENHANCE SELF-CONCEPT IN THE CLASSROOM. Englewood Cliffs, NJ: Prentice-Hall, 1976.

Centi, Paul J. UP WITH THE POSITIVE, OUT WITH THE NEGATIVE, Englewood Cliffs, NJ: Prentice-Hall, 1981.

Cordell, Franklin D., and Giebler, Gale R. TAKE 10 TO GROW. Niles, IL: Argus Communications, 1978.

Dodson, Fitzhugh. THE YOU THAT COULD BE. Chicago, IL: Follett Publishing, 1976.

Elkins, Dov Peretz. GLAD TO BE ME. Englewood Cliffs, NJ: Prentice Hall, 1976.

Fadiman, James. UNLIMIT YOUR LIFE. Berkeley,CA: Celestial Arts, 1989.

Frey, Diane, and Carlock, C. Jesse. ENHANCING SELF-ESTEEM, Muncie, IN: Accelerated Development, 1984.

Frisch, Ann, and Frisch, Paul. DISCOVERING YOUR HIDDEN SELF. New York: New American Library, 1976.

Greenwald, Jerry. BE THE PERSON YOU WERE MEANT TO BE. New York: Dell Publishing, 1973.

Hampden-Turner, Charles, and May, Rollo. WHO ARE YOU? Englewood Cliffs, NJ: Prentice-Hall, 1974.

Hooper, Doug. YOU ARE WHAT YOU THINK. New York: Prentice Hall, 1980.

Hulme, William. WHEN I DON'T LIKE MYSELF. New York: Popular Library, 1976.

Kennedy, Eugene. IF YOU REALLY KNEW ME, WOULD YOU STILL LIKE ME? Argus Communications, 1975.

Lembo, John. HELP YOURSELF. Niles, IL: Argus Communications, 1974.

Losoncy, Lewis E. TURNING PEOPLE ON . Englewood Cliffs , NJ: Prentice-Hall, 1977.

Maltz, Maxwell. PSYCHO-CYBERNETICS. New York: Warner Books, 1975.

THE MAGIC POWER OF SELF-IMAGE PSYCHOLOGY. New York: Pocket Books, 1974.

Maslow, A. H. TOWARD A PSYCHOLOGY OF BEING. New York: Van Nostrand Publishing, 1968.

May, Rollo. MAN'S SEARCH FOR HIMSELF. New York: Dell Publishing, 1953.

Montagu, Ashley. ON BEING HUMAN. New York: Hawthorn Books, 1966.

Moustakas, Clark E. TURNING POINTS. Englewood Cliffs, NJ: Prentice-Hall, 1977.

Newburger, Howard, and Lee, Marjorie. WINNERS AND LOSERS. New York: New American Library, 1974.

Newman, Mildred, and Berkowitz, Bernard. HOW TO BE YOUR OWN BEST FRIEND. New York: Ballantine Books, 1971.

Pollock, Ted. MANAGING YOURSELF CREATIVELY. New York: Hawthorn Books, 1971.

Samuels, Shirley C. ENHANCING SELF-CONCEPT IN EARLY CHILDHOOD. New York: Human Sciences Press, 1977.

Satir, Virginia. PEOPLEMAKING. Palo Alto, CA: Science & Behavior Books, 1972.

Simmermacher, Donald G. SELF-IMAGE MODIFICATION, BUILDING SELF-ESTEEM. Deerfield Beach, FL: Health Communications, Inc., 1981

Twerski, Abraham J. LIKE YOURSELF—AND OTHERS WILL TOO. Englewood Cliffs, NJ: Prentice-Hall, 1978.

Warner, Samuel J. SELF-REALIZATION AND SELF DEFEAT. New York: Grove Press, 1966.

Weinberg, George. SELF-CREATION. New York: Avon Books, 1978.

Wells, Joel. WHO DO YOU THINK YOU ARE? Chicago, IL: The Thomas More Press, 1989.

Williams, Richard J. I JUST MET SOMEONE I LIKE AND IT'S ME. New York: Sensory Research, 1976.

**FOR FURTHER INFORMATION ABOUT
GETTING A SELF-ESTEEM BUILDING
SEMINAR IN YOUR COMMUNITY, WRITE
DON SIMMERMACHER
7516 LA MADERA RD., NE
ALBUQUERQUE, NM 87109
(505)821-5564**

More Quality Books from R & E Publishers

THE COMPLETE CAREER HANDBOOK. by Dan J. McLaughlin. This information packed guide will give you everything you need to get the job you want. Written for first time job hunters and experienced workers re-entering the job market, this book will lead you through every phase of the job search.

Competition for good jobs is tougher than ever. Use this book to create the success you deserve.

$4.95	LC 91-50988	ISBN 0-88247-914-8
Trade Paper	6x9	Order #914-8

CURE YOUR MONEY ILLS: Improve Your Self-Esteem Through Personal Budgeting by Michael R. Slavit, Ph.D. Money is not the root of all evil, but the mishandling of it is a leading cause of emotional upheaval and marital breakups.This insightful work can help you to get control of your money and your life. Written by a psychologist who has taught money management techniques at the college level and in professional seminars, this book will help you to understand why you spend money the way you do and show you how to use it to meet your daily expenses, put aside money for vacations, save for a rainy day and be prepared for the occasional surprise monsoon.

$7.95	LC 91-50987	ISBN 0-88247-915-6
Trade Paper	6x9	Order #915-6

WHAT WORKS: 5 Steps to Personal Power by William A. Courtney. Life is simple—if you know *What Works* and what doesn't.

This power packed action guide is a handbook for creating your dreams. Based on time tested universal principles, this book will guide you through the five steps of personal power. Once you master these simple principles, you will be able to create anything you want, from better health, to financial success, to deeper, more loving relationships.

$7.95	LC 91-50983	ISBN 0-88247-910-5
Trade Paper	6 x 9	Order #910-5

THE GOAL BOOK: Your Simple Power Guide to Reach any Goal & Get What You Want by James Hall. Would you like to be able to turn your dreams into realities? You can if you have concrete goals. This book is based upon a unique goal achievement technique developed by a high school teacher and career counselor in California's Silicon Valley. "Action Conditioning Technology" (ACT) will help you convert your dreams and wishful fantasies into obtainable goals. With this new achievement technology, you will be able to decide exactly what you want, what steps you need to take and when you will reach your objective.

$6.95	LC 91-50675	ISBN 0-88247-892-3
Trade paper	6 x 9	Order #892-3

WORDS TO THE WISE: A Wonderful, Witty & Wise Collection of Good Advice on Life by Don Farias. Is life getting you down? Does it seem to be too much trouble to get out of the way of a speeding truck? Help is on the way with this collection of warm, funny and inspirational essays and poems.

You can read this book straight through, or savor it a section at a time, whenever you need a boost to get you out of bed and to motivate you to make every day better than the one before.

This book is the finest investment guide you can buy. It will help you spend your time and energy wisely so you can increase the value of your most important asset—your life. So take some words from the wise and read this book.

$6.95	LC 91-50691	ISBN 0-88247-897-4
Trade Paper	6 x 9	Order #897-4

THE SEARCH FOR MANHOOD: A Guide for Today's Men & Women by Scott Leighton. *What does it mean to be a man?* Men's roles are changing in our society. As women seek greater equality and power, men now look for greater depth and meaning. This collection of humorous and hard hitting essays will help men, and the women in their lives, to reach a greater understanding of what it really means to be a man. It examines the most vital issues in the lives of every man—work, family, sexuality, emotions and the legacy of boyhood. This pivotal work will help men to give themselves permission to feel and express the entire range of emotions, from love and anger, to joy and despair. It will release them from the bondage of socially imposed roles that have forced them to be only half alive.

$6.95	LC 91-50986	ISBN 0-88247-916-4
Trade Paper	6x9	Order #916-4

THE SOLUTION STRATEGY: Your Handbook for Solving Life's Problems by Phil McWilliams. If you didn't have any problems, what would you do? You'd probably be reading *The Solution Strategy* by Phil McWilliams. He has written the one book you need to solve *any* problem. Now you can stop relying on luck or guesswork to handle difficult situations. With this step-by-step technique you'll be able to determine where your problems come from, how to identify them and then—eliminate them. You'll learn how to overcome problems through the integration of emotions and intellect. Once you learn these techniques, you'll be able to accomplish any goal. *The Solution Strategy* is not Pop Psychology or Religion. It is a new kind of self-help book that really works!

$9.95	LC 91-61309	ISBN 0-88247-875-3
Trade paper	6x9	Order #875-3

YOUR ORDER

ORDER #	QTY	UNIT PRICE	TOTAL PRICE

Please rush me the following books. I want to save by ordering three books and receive FREE shipping charges. Orders under 3 books please include $2.50 shipping. CA residents add 8.25% tax.

SHIP TO:

(Please Print) Name: _____

Organization: _____

Address: _____

City/State/Zip: _____

PAYMENT METHOD

Enclosed check or money order

MasterCard   Card Expires _____   Signature _____

Visa

R & E Publishers • P.O. Box 2008 • Saratoga, CA 95070 (408) 866-6303 FAX (408) 866-0825